Lyrical
incantations

for the

criminally
insane

K.Z. Ponders

iUniverse

LYRICAL INCANTATIONS FOR THE CRIMINALLY INSANE

iUniverse books may be ordered through booksellers or by contacting:

iUniverse
1663 Liberty Drive
Bloomington, IN 47403
www.iuniverse.com
1-800-Authors (1-800-288-4677)

ISBN: 978-1-5320-7167-6 (sc)
ISBN: 978-1-5320-7168-3 (e)

Library of Congress Control Number: 2019912652

Print information available on the last page.

iUniverse rev. date: 09/13/2019

CONTENTS

DECA 4

DECA 5

Fade In

THE CHAINS

EXT: Supreme Court – Dusk

WE SEE a Chain Gang of convicted Souls exiting the courthouse doors.
Now exposed to the bitter cold of a Massachusetts wintery gust.

WE HEAR the wind and the rush. Causing the dark gray foliage to brush.

WE HEAR the rush and the rustle of ankle chains and handcuffs.
Standard Transportation gear.

WE FOCUS on our HERO bringing up the rear.
A chill of fear.
He shakes.
A warm tear on a cold face.
The warmth of such, ripples the gusts.
Crinkling the frost of winters touch.

Our HERO is thankful for this bitter Nor'easter.
For it shades his shakes.
His innocence.
His Terror.

SUPERIMPOSING his eye with a Dragon's Lair.
Smoke from a Dragon.
Exhaust, cover of a Paddy Wagon.
The Correction Officer opens the doors.

Correctional Officer:
(Grunt on his face)
Ain't no lollygagging!
Pick up those feet! I don't wanna
hear any of those chains a'dragging.
Oh, and watch your head
as you step into
this here Paddy Wagon.
Ok lady's, next stop, concrete cabin!

WE SEE our HERO enter in last.
The sound of Fleetwood Mac is blasting from the radio inside. It's hiding fear of anger and The Crucible of the awaiting stranger.

OUR HERO'S own family.
Now his stranger.
He catches a glimpse of his family.
Who are waving goodbye.
As they warm themself to the slowly culminating heater inside their car.

<u>OUR HERO</u>
Is that them?
Yes, that's them.
I think it is?
I think it's them.

With a smile and a kiss, blown by freedom's lips. The hard doors of the Paddy Wagon slam and click! And the climax bangs to Fleetwood Mac's chains. And this is how our story begins.

Lyrical Incantations for the criminally Insane.

THE QUEST FOR ZERO

Zero, what is zero?
Well, it's something that some people hold above all that is, and all that ever shall be.

Lost and drowning in the sea of continuous bliss, sweet nothings nothingness and
someone else's supporting kisses.
To that great abyss of the soul.
Sometimes zero can be cold,
and
sometimes zero can be hot,
and just when you think you've understood it.
You have not.

In our heart is this agápe passion.
Which should last until the end of all time,
but alas, people fall in and out of it
all the time.
Without rhyme or reason.
Another season,
another figure to Love.
As we try and shove
this overwhelming feeling
of unbridled consumption
of one another's
existence
aside.
Like an ever-changing tide.
It's something you can't hide from.
Because everybody wants some.
Like a bullet is to a gun;
so too is zero to someone.
Separately they work ineffectively,
but when put together they can be quite deadly.
Piercing through the lonely thoughts of non existence. Once it's absorbed the consistency of the two's
very substance
become a union of devotion and suspicion.
Separation is inevitable.
Either by death or departure.
For you see,

Yin's need to nurture
&
Yang's need to conquer.
An explosive mixture which burst through the seams of one's emotional state.

Due to this great collaboration of joy and pain; that flows through the veins releasing
this sweet sensation of endorphins and dopamine in our brain!
Thus causes us to go,
completely and utterly insane!
We will NEVER refrain from it,
Because it's just a bit of give-and-take.
So for heaven's sake.
You say,
what is zero?
I say to you, without a doubt, it's something we can't live width or width out.

TWO MASTERS

No one can serve two masters.
Because doing such would cause a disaster.
This is the quandary
I often find myself in.
Constantly think of my family.
This in turn,
distracts me.
From looking and learning
about what's around me.
I must focus my attention
here,
or
I won't get back to them there...
I must learn how to
block them.
In order to get back to them...
I must learn to forget them.
Sounds crazy.
Maybe?
But from here on out,
I will block them out.
Totally here.
Now aware of your master, son.
You shall Master.
The master of one.

OFF THE SUNSET STRIP

Pimp falls hard
on the boulevard.
Hearts get scarred
on the boulevard.

You better make your mark
on these streets.
Got the finest hoes
on these streets.

Heaven knows,
my ends stay meaty.
All my tens need me.

My dimes speak
frequently.
Pull trix
incrementally.

My fleet stay on fleek
indefinitely.
You feel me?
That hoe shine,
make me chic.

Those trix
rewind
spend time
His money, now mine.
See mine.
Nice watch.
Nice time.
Have mine or be mine.
Yeah man,
that used to always be my state of mind.
Way back, way back, back into time.

When my fine dime Dizzle,
bottom bitch sizzle,
had me fucked up like,
Wooh, this shit for rezzle.

You see my bottom bitch,
that's my heart.
I saved that child
from the Lost and The Dark.

Her moms was lost,
She was put on a cross.
Because of the cracks in her heart.
That crack she was smoking,
that crack smoke,man
that was the dark.
The love for her own child became
lost in her heart...

Then after awhile,
I guess I put that same child to work.

If you think about it,
It's really totally crazy berserk.

How I make it all work.
How it works, I guess.
How I make sense of it,
in my head.

I saved this child from
the lost and the dead.
Then put that same child
to work in
the land of the living dead.

How it does and how it doesn't.
And I was.
And I wasn't.
And I looked.

Man, she stunned me!
She stung me.
Like a honey bee.
As the rain fell abundantly.

Then suddenly it hit me!
Like sucking on Mama's tits bee.

This woman out there,
is the same woman who made me.

Maybe, I should just pick her up
in this whip, rite here.
Head for the bricks
off the Sunset Strip, I swear.

I do declare!

Like, it's just
me and you.
Everything else,
don't mean shit!

So, I pull up quick.
So my mind don't slip.

She flips.
As the rain falls,
she is trying to think of something quick.
I just smile and don't say shit.
She smiles back and hops in the whip. The rest is history
off the Sunset Strip.

JEZEBEL AFICIONADO

The enchanting air
of a sultry woman,
in stilettos.
Is quite the sight to behold.
Her scent,
sent my way
by a flirtatious breeze.
Oh,
what pleasures shall unfold
within those mysterious
beckoning eyes, untold.
I hold her near to me.
I become aroused by curiosity.
Promiscuity?
Rage and passion clash and blend!
Sweaty hands.
Hearts beat at a most feverish pace.
How I would love to taste, her.
Entrance way.
The slightest hint
of a salty violation.

                                    Yes.

An erection from my frustration.
She notices my excitement,
Smiles with devious delightment.
Because she loves to entice an erection,
no matter it's direction.

                          We kiss in anger.
            My mind haunted by this unreal stranger.
                        I pull her near,
                              in anger.

Closer.
        I pull her hair,
back.
Closer.
            I breathe
                a ton of adrenalin
            upon her neck, softly.

Tiny bites.
Listening.
Listening closely for the sounds of regrets.
In her sighs.
In those eyes.
Trying my best to uncover her lies.
Penetrating.
                              Deeper and deeper,
                                   into her soul.
               Wanting so much to know.
            The secrets of this harlot,
      never before told.
Finally...
She lets go,
          and lets me know,
                                        of her infidelity.
                    Instantly awakened.
            Awakened by the Forsaken.
I am for certain,
that this angry Love
is my burden.
Is our burden?
A burden we bear with loving care.
                    How do I love the honest err
                         of my
                    sweet Jezebel fair.

THE UNDYING FLAME OF
THE SYMBIOTIC SOULS

A thousand points of light.
Has led
to the
intersection
of
you and I.
Where the forces of us
collide and combine
from the
slightest touch.
The rush of such.

Goosebumps appear.
A standing ovation
of tiny hairs.
Here, there,
and everywhere.
A single stare.
A ubiquitous kiss
set us adrift.
Set ablaze,
we become
the night
and the day.
Gravitate.
Levitate.
Penetrate.
We began to
meditate.
Then radiate.
Reflecting
the passion we make.
Now engaged.
Now enraged,
The mighty Sun
Of

the day
is jealous of us
for stealing his praise.
Fueled by rage.
The mighty Sun
intensifies his rays.
Feeling the heat,
we go separate ways.
A self-inflicted grenade.
Neither one of us
comfortable in the shade.
A choice made.
A choice given.
Lost and searching
for something
we've always had.
Better off dead
than to live without the other.
One thing leads to the other.
We discover,
that somehow
we were lovers,
even before,
we ever even,
met each other.
As fate would have it.
We were back at it.
like rabbits.
But,
It's more than that...
it's like a habit.
It's like,
we gotta have it.
Like Oxygen to breathe.
We are what we need.
She the flower and I the seed.
The ground
on which we stand is now stronger
Hand in hand.
Forsaking the plans
of all those
who choose to oppose
<u>The undying flame</u>
<u>of the</u>
<u>symbiotics souls</u>.

THE DAY THE HOT DOG
LOST HIS KNISH

The confusion was great that day.
As it clouded the Empire State a certain way. Many say, the haze was due to the blaze that the knish
factory made.
Leaving our beloved red hot to have not his potato side counterpart.

Lost, bewildered, and in the dark.
Sadly, we approached the Metropolitan Street carts with this heartfelt loss. We witnessed our water
dog placed in his bun with mustard and kraut,
but without his crispy mashed delicacy for company.
Oh, how we relished palatal symmetry. Frankly, they used to be
the edible Majesty of New York City.

The snappy sog of the dog.
The slight tinge mingled about from the sauerkraut, and then my friends,
the crispy whipped bliss of that potato knish.
Kissed with just the right hint of spiciness from the mustard, golden brown.

Wash it all down with an ice cold
Dr. Brown's black cherry or cream.
It was all part of the
supreme dream cuisine.
Then the knish vanished!

Leaving us famished and our hot dog unbalanced.

Walking through the entrance of Katz's Delicatessen.
Stressing, and crestfallen with my head hanging low...
But wait?
What's that I smell?
Lo and behold I smell, potato?
Yes!
Yes, the potato knish is back in full effect!

The aroma Ambrosia is on the grill right next to its favorite weiner.
Who seems to be grilling with a grin.

The Schnitzel has his friend and
all Is right in the big city once again.

The End.

FIDELITY IS LAME

Fidelity is lame.
I much rather enjoy
the strange deranged
pain from the suspicion game.
That sweet bitter heat
from a lying cheat.
Who is so discreet.
When and where
they meet.
Her rendezvous with god-knows-who.
What can I do about
her mischievous ways?
Cut her head off and run through a maze.
Lost In a daze from
her comfortable gaze.
Her comfortable ways.
My heart set ablaze.
Phone calls she makes,
and receive some parts unknown.
The Dark Side of dawn.
Unanswered rings from an AM phone.
Making my mind spin
and my heart race.
Putting me in the zone.
Her sweet voice.
A muffled tone.
A gron.
Periodic sounds of a
dishonest liaison.

She tells me it's only the TV.
My overactive imagination.
Overactive Sensations.
Over-acting her negotiations.

Delusions of an invisible stranger.
Aroused by the danger.
Stranger and stranger.

Why am l delighted
by such a
perverse delusion.

A childhood,
I assume,
where Mother's Love was confusing.

Misplacing love for pain.
This changed my brain.
Feeding this pain with lust!

Plus, many hours have passed since I heard from her last.

Rock hard and teeth gnashed.
Then suddenly,
she appears before me.
Hair mashed.
Clothing tattered and mismatched.

I ravage her with the clash
of joy and suspicion!
Right here in the kitchen!
On the ground we lay twitching.
Enthralled in ecstasy from my pain.
Yes, my friends,
fidelity is quite lame,
quite lame indeed.

20 GRAMS

20 grams is the essence of man.
A measurement in grams.

20 grams is the weight of the Soul,
or so I'm told.

20 grams is the weight of
all the stories ever ever told.

20 grams less after your body
turns cold cold cold.

20 grams of a living soul,
but can 20 grams understand though?
A bold question if you know what I know.
The heavy your soul gets.
The heavier your controls.
A heavy souled Alchemist.
A religious forbidden resistance.
The 20 grams believed to be consistent.
The Alchemist is persistent.
   • Chromosomal division
   • Separation
   • Evolution
More than 20 grams is the ultimate conclusion.

How can we make something weigh more than something we don't even understand?
All the more.
More for sure.

The Rebirth of Another Earth

Another Earth is born
in the sacred vessel of Mother birth.
The cream soda soldiers of virility pop with a sizzle. Then make their way through the many obstacles
of Her Majesty.
Hoping for a miracle and willing to give their lives in the hopes that that miracle comes true.
For me and you.
This is how our tree begins.

With a mighty swim of hope.

A frenzied journey set to motion with a great explosion.

Out of many we are one.

One is chosen.

A notion is perceived.

A notice is the creed.

And the sacred vessel awaits its seed.

The chosen penetrates its destination.

The destiny of obligation.

The seed of life has now begun.

The egg of life is our schematic plan.

This is the Master Plan

of division and addition.

Contractions and reactions.

A miracle in fractions.

Whirling dervish.

Galactic chromosomal reactions.

They crash in and divide.

Then they combine.

The divine creation.

Evolution of intelligent design.

The golden ratio of mankind.

This design is the Caduceus intertwined throughout the whole of the universe.

From the first to the last.

The present, future, and the past.

All is cast within the flower of life.

The sacred rite of the water burst.

Now another Earth shall be pushed forth through the spiritual stargate.

The great entryway Vesica Pisces.

Her Majesty,
Mother Earth,
once again gives birth
to a planetary being.
Who then will search for meaning.
Because... seeing is believing.

THE SECOND TRIMESTER

Convolutedly conceived by unwanted conception.
A thought begins from unused contraception.
Incestuous Inception.
Incubation to the second trimester.
My life is considered a disaster.
The bastard child of a family playing dumb.
A miracle to some,
yet others consider me a cancer.
I have no say in the second trimester.

ODYSSEY INCARCERATUS

Minute one:
Heavy barred doors slam with a jam!

Lunch is pasteurized
eggs and turkey ham.
I don't want turkey ham!
I don't want turkey ham Uncle Sam,
in this Jungle of man.

Ain't nowhere to sit.
So I just stand.
Covering my six.
Looking pissed and listless,
but rock like rigid.
Sometimes when I'm nervous I start to fidget.
At my nine is a Mexican midget.
He's smoking a spliff.
My eight is laughing.
He's just joking.
It ain't shit.
Then my one says something.
Next second I noticed.
Eight, no laughing.
Silencio.
Then it just happened.
8 to 1
They get to clapping.
My seven is Shifty quick to my one.
He got a nice buck-fifty.
Terracotta Red and blue blood
sailing to the ceiling.
The Bullpen railing.
The C.O pulled the pin around 8:11.

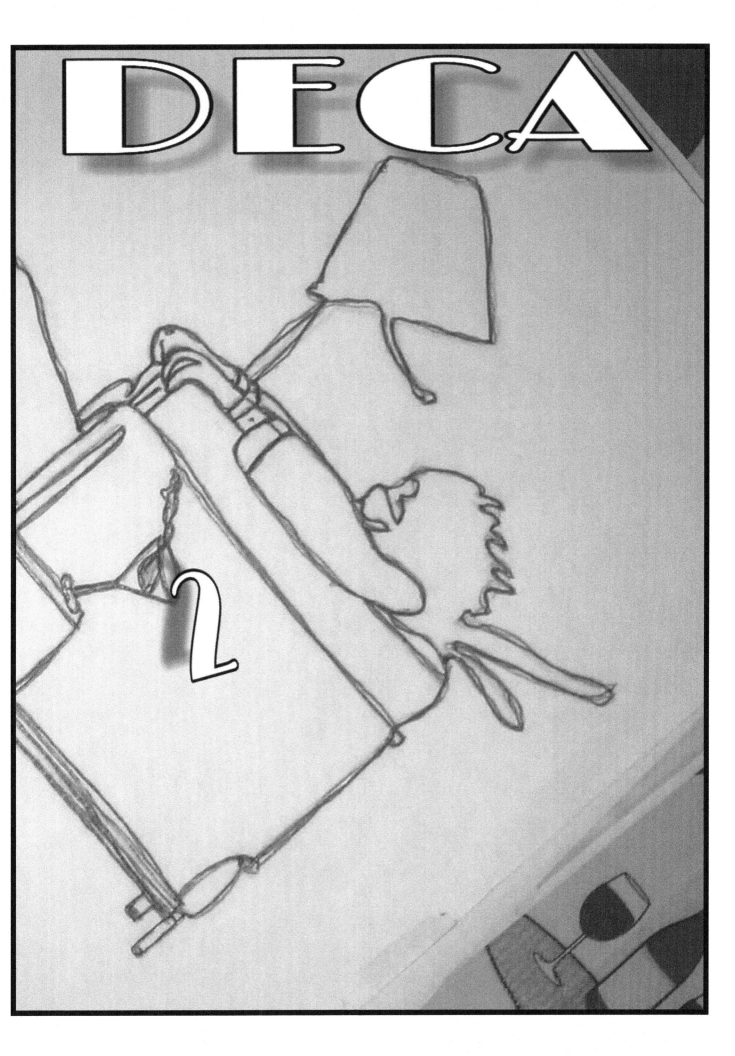

HOW TO ESCAPE AN EGG

First, it must be said,
that in the beginning,
it was a nice little place to rest my head.

Then my head
became full of lead.
Then swollen red.
It became too big for that egg I was in.
So a mission was led
from without & within.
I became bigger and outgrew my skin,
I was in.

                The umbilical mind of original sin.

Cut.
Severed.
Snipped off forever.
Mazel Tov!

                Fill your head.
                Escape the egg,
                and live forever…

If you're clever.

COMPOS MENTIS

Δ
Let us begin,
where it all began.
In the brain stem
where we gather
i. n. f. o. r. m. a. t. i. o. n.

Waiting in our enclosure,
called the womb,
with
anticipation.
Somatosensory cortex
sensations
release motor cortex
stimulations.
Thalamus interpretations,
of said
sensations and stimulations,
reverberate neural synergy from neural transmitting energy.
Oscillating the continuity
of
our
vivacious consciousness.™
A
neural plasmic
metamorphosis
has already begun.
In the cerebrum,
where contemplation comes from.
There is a labyrinth of learning when your mind is turning. While it turns
oooooO. .it yearns for more. .Oooooo
When you are willing to
o p e n u p t h a t d o o r,
your corpus collosum
will no longer

endure the separation.
Interpretation of
hemispheric

negotiations.

Therefore, your brain.
will give way and
your mind, this mind

will stay
forevermore.

Forevermore,
in the perpetual
expansion of contemplation!
A pine cone
evolution evaluation.
Simply by accepting
this possibility.
We connect
to the
quantum
reality
of the
seen
and
unseen.

THE QUESTION MARK KILLER

This is the story of the question mark killer.
Who lurks in the shadows of one's own mind.
Plaguing mankind with the hard to find.
Interweaving reality with paranoia and doubt.
So much so that the victims shout and frantically move about.
Because they cannot figure IT out.
You see, it starts as a whisper then festers into the crooked shapes of the killers' works...
Spawning one, to go absolutely berserk.
Many have fallen, and many have perished, and many have lost all that they have cherished.
The ways of the killer have been proven for eons.
As I stand upon the very edge, of this very ledge, succumb by the mystery.

This pledge I pledge unto thee...
Trust me, dear fellows, that what I say is true.
Worry not, about your quandaries.
For the answer is just ahead of thee.

But if you choose to question this warning,
then the killer has already gotten to you,
and there's nothing more I,
or even you
can do,
now,
but...
Jump! Jump, along with me.
Atop this magnificent height,
and splatter upon

The hard concrete
of
paranoid reality.™

Then we will crack.
Let's jump.
There's no turning back.

THE HYMEN OF THE MIND

Here, in the fullness of empty space
                              do I find my true religion.
                                  Our minds pulsate
                                      to the same
                                      frequencies
                                         as the
                                   spinning earth.

In the frequencies of unity.™
                           Electromagnetic stimulations of
                                this butterfly effect,
                                   with the sacred
                             right and left hemispheres
                                  of the universe.

Born in God's image was you, was I,
young Jedi.
It's image in our eye
An image beyond the sky.
Neuro transmitted sunlight
travels the interstellar spaces of the
Celestial cortex.
Gray matter Dark matter.
Light matter vortex.
Creating anatomically correct planetary systems of tangible imagination in the
                              neuronic galaxy.™
Where we, and the creator, are one.
The atom, is the Eve neuroplastic evolution.
A supernova of sensations has already changed what once was, to what now is.
Now is,
the event horizon.
Any further, and you will be contorted into the synapses of multi-dimensional parallel realities.
Releasing the dopamine of let there be...
Light from the nebulous of a big bang conception.
Ejaculated revolutions.
                            The parthenogenesis
                                     of
                                actuality.™
An idea is formed. A star is born.

                              Before it happens.
                     It has already happened.
I hereby give notice, read everything,
Know further.
                              Immaculate perception.
Now you are officially deflowered.
Was it as good for you as it was for me?
Well, I guess, I'll just have to wait and see.

AND IT CAME TO PASS

And it came to pass,

that the pilgrimage of Jesus eventually led him to wander the Wilderness to search for Bliss and a broader sense of what his mission really is all about.

As he wandered he wondered.

Then doubt sprang a thunder.

Lo and behold,

He came upon the first begotten

of the Great Wonder,

the Serpent Asunder.

Whose castration from heaven

was set at the trial of 7 times 77.

"Show mercy upon the desiccation of this location,

and summon

The Angel Vegetation

to Spring forth and give mastication,

to this starving population."

The Serpent tries to implant a temptation.

Jesus replies with the wink of his eye.

"It is not I who decides

the feast or the famine.

For I am the son of

the fruitful King,

I am.

Sent by him, ad rem,

to excavate the weeds of sin.

While cultivating the seeds of them who breathe in him, and all shall feed again and again from without & within.

"Well, allow me to retort,"

                    says The Serpent of Sin.

"Inter alia inter alios, host of host?

Whom, what, and when, has thou

come to save...again?

Are we all not enslaved by the grave,

my friend?"

Jesus now dismayed.

He starts to question the answer he gave.

As they went their way in the heat of the day.

The sweltering rays give way and start to sway.
A hue of transition lay.
Resurrecting a dust cascade which mingles with the shade of an old man's grave.

The Serpent therein surveyed,
and thus sayed.

"Have I not read,
that the universe is made of you,
of us and of them?
All that is of God and Men.
A multiverse in reverse
from without & within?
Death,
this then be the worst curse my friend.
Is it the righteous consequence of sin?"
The Serpent pointing toward the gravestone.
"Inverse this old man's curse
and permit him to rise again."
And then Jesus wept and said;
"Upon this man's head the
celestial Serafin shall forever glorify the dead. The Gates of Heaven extend,
and he shall live again.
Betwixt-and-between
the quantum strings
that connect
All Things to all things.
Oscillating to the frequency of Harmony. Blessed Be he.
In vivo beatus ab initio.
He, the regenerated soul,
who holds the answers for Thy,
of who, what, when, and why."
Stupefied and fascinated,
The Serpent Asunder stood
silently debilitated.
As the winds about them violently altercated.
Allocated by a whirling Shaitan.
They become spirited far beyond
the bonds of Rue.
The dark aged voodoo adieu.
The swirling and whirling,
this chaotic Shaitan, alight the two upon
a strange place anew.

The Alterview Bleu.
A peculiar Oasis where characteristics
seem to trade places.
Then,
there at the river trade races.
The Serpent Asunder begins to
feel strange spaces of it's cerebral.
Seems as though it's laced with...
Tranquility.
The great beguiler becomes
beguiled by humility.
A saving grace soliloquy started from within fester within the Beast, you see,
and it begins to see,
and feel things much much differently.
A true blue epiphany.
Suddenly,
The Serpent believed that Jesus,
only Jesus, has the ability to absolve
it's pregnancy iniquity.
Immediately The Serpent Asunder kneels before it's Messiah.
Praying forgiveness from the mire eternal fire.
"Is it greater to be the grandsire of the boastful Abyss,
or a humble servant of the heavenly bliss?"
With this, now having been said.
Twilight mist kenosis changing everything from bleu to red.
Then the shadow of Jesus intensifies by the shade of the Serpent.
The shadow of Jesus multiplies
a thousand times its original size.
Revealing a darker side to this starry night and the most holy Christ.
Interosculation of his mission and it's plight.
Divination of wrongs and rites.
Awareness awakens.
Thus, nullifying the forever forsaken.

"Upon the sacrifice for original sin,
that which thou hast delivered unto them,
you Satan shall be forgiven.
Relieving thee of the thy transgressions.
Yet, you shall forever preside over hell
and also serve our beloved Father as well.
You shall serve as
the adversary of humanity.
The polarity to his Majesty.
Now, away with thee!
Vade retro, satana!"

Here now, Angelic Minstrel.
Release the ghost of present past/
Liberate the looking glass/
Understanding how/
your cast was casted/
this shall make the first one last/
Good God Almighty be free at last.

THE GREATEST GAME
EVER PLAYED

Hurry! Hurry! Step right up.

Come and see the greatest game ever played.

You will, I guarantee

be truly mesmerised and hypnotized

by the amazing true lies

told by The Man from behind the curtain.

Best be for certain,

that you will believe every word said.

Because this man has a way of getting straight through, right into your head.

Hurry! Hurry!

Come and be beguiled by

The Great Seductress and most beloved Enchantress, the most alluring, Propagandist. Who WILL fill your mind with so much misinformation you will neither have the.   CapaCity or the AudaCity, to question any

Of the Implications.

Yes, yes Ladies Ladies and Gentlemen.

The game whimsical ways will have you amazed and dazed to the point that you will believe whatever we saying, Arrière pensée,

The things behind the things we say.

Step right up, and behold a most magnificent media show.

we will preach and teach you,

doom and gloom.

Here nor there yet it is everywhere.

Apocalyptic lipstick coming to you live and direct from a television room!

Then there's the old witch's broom.

Known to me and you, my friends, as scripted reality TV.

Come and be, bewitched by the idiot box.

Giving you all you need, and would ever want to see. Believe you me?

Everything, from ignorant drama to the puppet of change, President Obama.

CIA drama for Prince William's party disguised as a comic Bin Laden was naughty.

Now change his Fame, and we play the Trump game.

Yes, ladies and gentlemen, do you see what I mean? Can you see past the dream. All the schemes and all the players are present before you. Wait, wait don't walk away yet. I'll try not to bore you. We truly adore you and would never ignore you. Feeling down depressed and under the weather? Take an advertisement. I swear, you'll feel much, much better.

And now ladies and gentlemen,

The Mysterious Magicians, the Politicians.

They will trick you into believing that your votes really count. They all go out and move about. Speaking on the behalf of things that don't exist, yet. With a slight of hand and the flick of the wrist. They get you to believe that YOU really give a shit. For, even when their losing they win, no matter the voting count, recount or any such decision.

The Splendid vision. Immaculate perception.

MK Ultra Magic

and the

Frantic Fanatics

Kalvin Klein's Obsession, for men and women. It's your decision. It's a split decision. Peer pressure static.Meow Mix anime graphics. We use for terroristic tactics. The C.I.A man and his Advertising Genius.

figure it out.

Yes, ladies and gentlemen,

The terrorists that work for men.

You will always love it again and again!

And last but not least, for our game, no game would not be complete. Unless, we introduce you to the great and powerful, voodoo Gurus, or better known as the religious crew. The things they say and the things we do. Watch very closely. You're watching a master. They are already inside of you Thinking our way. Without thinking, you'll quickly be sinking into the quicksand. Excuse me ma'am are you in need of a hand? Assistance? Resistance? Persistence? Of those who claim to be protected by God's hand? Come, come now don't be an odd fellow.

"Where are all the freaks, in this freak show?"

Oh, you still don't know.

You are the freaks.

We are all the freaks.

They are the freaks.

Because, we all allow it to be, so.

We are the creators of this maze.

All its players and its plays?

That's why it's,

The Greatest Game Ever Played.

THE SPIDER

The Most Benevolent Binary
Grand Arachnid.   Creator

&

Curator

of the Worldwide grid.

Digital venom injected.

Algorithmia effective

Ads accepted.

Scientifically selected.

Excessive similarities.

Homogenized mass hysterical revelries.

Confectional seminaries

and

habitual haberdasheries.

The preordained keystroke keys predicting

[Codex Consortium Cryptology]

Hot wet Teens!

[Retina mining recognizing technology]

01010100101NSA00101001001

Trojan Horse Datacare.

The eyes of The Spider are everywhere,

feeling vibrations with tiny hairs.

Like I said, I really like, taking pics of me and all my friends,

and all the really cool places we have been.

Then

The stuff

we're like really really into.

Since you don't really know

like really coolplacestogo

unless the computer tells you so.

#Imustgo! #Imustgo! Take pictures.

Be seen. Cause my smartphone is

Blinking I must go where it says so.

and so   the story goes

The Spider

who controls.

DO THE HUSTLE

It's about noon.
Just woke up.
Jumped in the whip.
It's time to hustle up.
So I dip looking for car dents to fix.
Hit the Wash and the parking garage.
Then I spot it.
A perfect quarter panel hit.
Straight suction cup shit.
What's that I see?
The owner of the car is still sitting in it, sweet!
I pull up quick in my whip, but with a real smooth demeanor.
Excuse me sir, I noticed your car is in need of repair, and if you like,
I can fix it right here.
Because today, is the day, that I'm off the shop.
Before he can says a word.
I already got my trunk popped.
You see sir, I have all the equipment that we require.
And at the same time I can save you from a higher insurance rate.
So while the owner contemplates, evaluates, and litigate.
But wait...Then pop!
Your dent is out, sir.
His car repaired.
The guy shouts "Wow!
Looks like new again"
See I told you what I can do, my friend.
On the spot body shop right here in the parking lot.
Tip on top, if you please.
Then the guy hands me eight 50s plus two tens.
A nice ice breaker.
Need just One more before I go in.
Then,
Excuse me? I was just watching
the way you fix that car.
Can you fix mine too?
It's really not too far from here.
Sure can my dear.
It's no trouble at all.
Doing the hustle.
Having a ball.

ON THE OTHER HAND

Storefront Neons Buzz.

As a crystal ball gleams with the tale of lost love.

The fortune teller declares an envious case of knotted hair.

The evil eye it seems is the cause of her client's broken dreams.

A sprig of mint and a dread of red placed under your pillow when you go to bed.

Now place the money in my hand and go your way in good faith my man.

Then on the other side of the storefront partition the fortune teller's family waits for food in the kitchen.

Her husband is upstairs trying to make his next very important decision.

What shoes look best when he goes out with the boys drinking.

His wife now, making food for the family.

An envelope waiting to be delivered.

Her husband now kisses her.

The envelope is delivered.

Now she is The Giver.

Have you ever considered a fortune teller's family?

Not some mythical story but a real life entity.

Just the same as you and me.

Just with the slightest bit of predictability.

The fortune teller is anonymity.

The best work she's ever done is for her family.

She is the foundation and the very fruits that bear upon her family tree, and yet she stays quiet and in the background completely devoted and dedicated to her family.

While her husband wears the mighty golden crown.

The house is quiet now.

The kids are to bed.

The neons are off.

Metropolitan city streets make their sound

as the lights go down.

The Fortune teller Smiles knowing that she is the strength of a Nation.

3 A.M.

3 in the morning,
woke up from a dream,
then these concrete walls,
yeah man,
they started to breathe.
I realize that this life ain't exactly what it seems. Wait just a minute...
I just had to sneeze.
True as this moment,
wearing prisoner green.
Too much to handle,
my nose starts to bleed.
life and its meaning,
and what does it mean?
And just for a moment.
I started to think...of what I was
just dreaming of.

ODYSSEY INCARCERATUS

Year One:
Eventually,
it seems clear,
that I am stuck in here.
Here for the long run,
to nowhere.
In nowhere.
Anywhere, everywhere!
Anywhere, but here.Try not to stare to hard. Back of my mind I'm praying to G-D.
Guy over there screaming for GOD.
Seems to be high in the hair of another man's derriere.
I couldn't tell you for sure.
I really didn't see it. Sometimes if you know too much you'll be the one that their seeing.
Or that other cat in the corner what tourette's disorder,
putting in his order for the next
gang related Slaughter.
Word on the street
it's going to be a riot.
I.C.E at the border,
Okay this is how we stay fly, kid.
First we start the riot.
Then we make it quiet.
Okay, light the pilot, spark it up and try it.
Now, sunsets over Horizons.
Eyes darken.
Dude, I.C.E grilling me.
Downright begging me to split him to the white meat.
Solitary food Eye now eat.
No release. No please. You can't even pray on your knees.
No homo Niger please.
No Understanding for hands and feet.
And this be

The Psycho Psychology

of

The Penitentiary

: Doppelganger of Society :

DREAMSCAPE DIVINE

In the hour of proper time
the subconscious mind meets
conscious rhyme.
A limelight like shine.
Herein,
the Dreamscape divine.
Conscious
Subconscious,
and, Unconscious.
We the Mind,
shine rewind.
The glare of
Starry Night Skies.

Herein, The Dreamscape Divine.
Alchemical Sunshine,
We reflex the Mind's Eye.
Dancing on photons.
Nocturnal Sunshine.

The Angelic Graces.
Ambien spaces.
Intertwining divinity.

Herein, The Dreamscape Divine.
Mnemonic pheromones of chemically charged cognition.
Releasing the place of Heaven's Gate.
We, D.M.T.
Alterwake.
Allocate.
Often The Cauldron of Dreams is rather Mystikal it seems. Or is it simply.
A recreations of the senses? Put together by nonsenses. Nonsense?
There is much to be learned from the alternate realm known to us as dreams. We are the creators.
We are the Essence. The dreams are our means by that which we create. Herein the Infinite Space
of the Dreamscape Divine.

THE MASTER OF SATAN

Once upon a choice I made,

Mephistopheles appeared unto me, at the foot of my bed, as I laid.

The beast leaned over to me and gently whispered in my ear,

these words you are about to hear:

"I am the one they call Lucifer, who bears the light, come to give understanding of a wrong, and make it right"

Now this grew hesitation in my soul. Knowing what I know.

For I all ways have been told that

Old Nick and his tricky tricks will lead you astray. Thoughts I thought, and then

I say:

"Beelzebub! Be gone, be on thy way!"

"Please, master may I stay."

The devil said with a humble face.

"Why have you called me master, and asked for my permission to stay here, in this place?"

"I am the one they call the Fallen star.

Cast out of heaven afar, to be here, where you are. The reason for my dismissal, you see, is that I refuse to bow down before thee.

For you are the master of me."

How could this be?

I whispered to myself.

The wealth from this information had me confused, and yet at the same time,

I must say, I was rather amused.

So I permitted the prince of darkness to continue it's song and dance.

For I might gain the chance to glance into the bittersweet romance of happenstance.

The cause and effect of the things we accept and those we reject...

"Neglect me not!

For, I am, the one they call Baphomet.

Who was given charge by the Almighty, so as to tempt thee. To test the loyalty.

To see, if you are truly who you say you be. Now, if you understand me?

You will be able to see more clearly.

You will be able to see calamity as it is truly meant to be."

And with that, It vanished into infinity...

Once again, I whispered words.

Trying my best to wrap my head around all I have just heard. Trying to turn words into verbs.

Then suddenly...

I became disturbed, by a great doom from across the room. My glass stem, you see, was staring rite back at me.

Thickly glazed brown and black from my many, many, cracks of yesteryear.

I should hit that rite now and make it sizzle. Just a bit.

I'd feel so good. I'd feel so lit.

Na, man, I don't want that shit! Oh shit, here it comes. What a tasty delight. Where's my lighter?

Where is the fuckin' light!?

Wait! I can't! This is my plight.

Fight the urge? Resist the splurge?

I can master the beast. At least

at the very least, for a little while.

This is simply a trial. A test.

I must do my best.

Put my mind to rest, and thunk.

And after awhile,

it was as though I were drunk without the drink. Simply by thinking of the power from within, I became free of my sin.

Now, and now all I do is win.

All thanks to Satan, and that night I let him in.

LUNACY OF THE MORNING STAR

A name.

A name.

What's in a name, if that name is the same to explain the fame of the Messiah and the Daemon?

Same name Same meaning. How deceiving. The lunacy, you see,

is with the title

The Morning Star,

which is by far more way bizarre.

Because that moniker is given to

Jesus and Satan.

How could this happen?

Someone caught napping, I assume.

For centuries no one, but no one has ever noticed this huge elephant in the room.

How could two polar personalities be anointed with the same name?

Who is to blame for a misleading name?

Misnomer fame.

Confusing the game.

Confusing the players.

Confusing my head with all of these layers.

Naysayers, may believe that this is of no importance.

But when it comes to the concordances in the history of Fate, which one shall I find before it's too late.

The one, or the other.

Or maybe, just maybe they might just be brothers.

Brothers who point to their father,

Which is even more odder than the name of the Martyr.

In The Honor of all those who opposed the crooked toes.

NARCOTIC NANCY

Who takes the world from Colorful Girls, and closes them tightly in medicine bottles?
Exquisite you. Now an exquisite skew.
Now slightly Askew.
Causing the Weebles & Wobbles.
Caught, captured, and, capsulated.
Full to the rim with empty emotional bottles.
Pure trance Mizuno.
Their children longing for a swaddle.
Wrapped in a mausoleum of gravy.
She once was a princess, a lady.
Now, She's all fucked up and batshit crazy. Her babies watch her babies.
Narcotic Nancy has a Pharmaceutical Fancy
for colorful Dandies. Living her life In perpetual fantasy.
Her children In perpetual amnesty.
This Is the life of Narcotic Nancy and an open bottle of colorful candy.
The baby is crawling over to kiss mommy.

A ROMANCE IN BLACK & BLUE

Hear about the Tree of Life, which matures upon the noble ground of stars and stripes.

Live two kind of fowl amid all the free birds,

the free birds of flight.

These two types just happened to be.

The Blackbirds And the Blue Jays.

It seems to me that they bicker and bicker and bicker rather frequently. One might say that to be at odds are their destinies.

For both of these birds have been manipulated from their infancy to believe the other a threat, you see. Implementations by the powers-that-be. Using their lives to create

clarity and confusion. A performing art of distraction and delusion. Eclipsing the exploits of what they're really doing.

Screwing with the faculties of illusionary enemies. Now, the Blue Jay's integrity is to

serve and protect, all the freebirds, none shall they reject and or neglect. Unfortunately they've been trained, albeit subconsciously, to look at the Blackbird suspiciously and quickly without question. Caught captured and kept in cages. And I must say, in an outrageous, endangerous, degree. Or maybe even worse, displayed in a hearse. Living the Blackbirds to believe that they have been cursed, unprotected, and neglected.

Wondering why blackbirds can't fly free?

Now, because of this strife the Blackbirds are leery of their own home. Their own tree.

A seed has been planted.

Division now granted.

Enchanted by the dramatics of the Blue Jays

antics. When the scene becomes frantic both sides start to panic. Leading to actions that are far from pragmatic. The situation is such that the Blackbirds perceive the Blue Jays to be corrupt.

"Sit down and shut up!"

The Blue Jays believe that

The Blackbirds are filthy, and thus must be, automatically guilty. Consequently, one will receive an acquittal. While the other will be permitted to be recidivated.

Naturally, this may lead to infractions, miscommunications, and frustration. A Total breakdown of civilization. When the protector

is the reason for the frustration.

Equivocation?

This is the tale repeated again and again.

Without end.

A story for the birds. Which might have sounded absurd. But if you closely observed it, we just might learn how to reverse it. Freedom?

TELEVISION BRAIN EATER

In a world...

Where vision and sound coagulate and all the people congregate at the pixelated altar. Minupulady. Viral sensation.

The Great Hullabaloo.

We the poltergeist children of Paradise cove are all aglow and watching the television snow. The tunnel visions insomniac creature feature show. No need to adjust your vision.

For we control the vertical and the horizontal.

While the audience performs like puppets dancing our advertising mambo.

         and away we go.

But wait there's more...

THE COLD CALL BLIZZARD

Now is the winter of my disconnect.

Never shall I look back.

Never shall I regret.

My retreat from the internet, and all its whimsical ways.

Daze and daze go by as time flies.

My eyes wide shut, to the world around me.

An Orwellian orgies filling every orifice with cookies.

Cookies! And more cookies!

Phishy Facebook friends who gather information.

Constant contact negotiations who hunger for my participation.

Deals! and savings! and deductions! from every direction!

All this happening in my direction.

To my discretion.

With pinpoint precision as to my location.

A Spectacula Dracula.

Draining a fella's fellowship with the significant other.

Why even bother, when all I need is up my sleeve. Like magic, the latest greatest object...

Which is now obsolete.

Intrinsic obsolescence, born to be replaceable.

Incomprehensible!

Wasteful!

Distasteful!

I here,

have had my fill!

That's why I sigh when a train or a bus goes by. Because all the peoples minds eyes are glued to the big surprise of a cat who cries, human tears.

Who cares! No really who cares?

Yet, you stare, I stare, we stare!

Who would dare question the cuteness of a cat who cries human tears?

I am aware of the advantages of technological advancements. Yet I still believe that the next step in the evolution of mankind, is not of technological advancements, but of advancements in the mind.

A dynamic equilibrium.

                            The idiom of the Elysium.

The illusion of the...   ‡6†6‡

                            < 6 >

                             U

Act now!

This is a limited time offer!

(Special conditions may apply)

Pay first ask questions later.

VULGAR REPERTOIRE

In the beginning there was a (thought%)
This therefore, brought about
E= hf = hc/λ. (h = 6.626★10-34 1e+ +here B= 💡
The Big_1,099,511,627,776 bytes Bang!)
Now (v) in your mind is a microcosmic universe, and as we traverse through the
macrocosmic universe.
This mind's force is our source, is the source of the creation. As we think we create, and the world
in which we created creates the thoughts we think-
Take a minute and let that sink in.
It's okay I'll wait.

```
        ?ïïïïiiiiiiWiiiiiïïïïïï¿
     —{( • )}—Δ—{( • )}—
         ( ~√\ ~ )
         ( # Ÿ # )
      `\____-____/;
```

Okay now you we ready?
Hold On steady. We may get a little slippery.
Cause from here on out it gets a little tripp.
Religion, all religion is an inspiration
of the mind. Tring to make sense of mankind.
Neither one is right or wrong.
Yet all should be equivalent as if they sing the same song.
= _¶_√_¶ =
{___¢___}:: @ ★†★ 1+1=3
   ★★ ★★

The glorious symphony of contemplation.™
Using our thoughts as navigations.
Moving from weigh station to weigh station.
The infinite process of education.™
This too, is the process of science.
Which is not contradictory by the least, from religion, but rather form an alliance.

Science
being the physical,
and religion the metaphysical.
Coincidentally,
you will see,
if you study,
the many are all one.

Now, I know many have been taught to choose a side, but why choose a side?

But why? What do they have to hide?

Why should one limit the process of the infinite mind?

Trying to hide from the illumination side?

Imagine if the world revolved around you. U

Imagine if you were perfection through and through. O

Imagine if your thoughts were able to conceive. {•̀•}•••Δ

Imagine that you just really believed.

$$1+1=3$$

!!!9!!!   /

Imagine how easily we are deceived.

    " !!!1!!!   /—¢

    " !!!1!!! <(°•°•°•°•°)√.com

    " !!!2!!!   ~~W~~—¢

    " !!!0!!!   ~~W~~

   +!#0#!+   ~~W~~

Now imagine I'm a liar, and that I should be set on fire.

Now you'll understand my desire.

THE CRUX OF MARY JANE AND THE MASONIC KING WITH NO NAME

One day while smoking on a spliff, I sat back and thought, and my mind came up with this shit...

The sacred geometry and symbolic symmetry

of the 9/11 malignancy is quite a staggering sight to see... and understand. Or try to begin to understand the master plan.

The Grand Design of Man.

Man's plan, or God's prophecy?

Now, let me enlighten thee to the sacred mysteries of this so called "evil illuminati".

At the front plaza, where the Towers once stood. There was a golden sphere with black inside, Mecca implied. The designer's guide,

the divine divide or the golden section.

This then, is the brotherhood. Which are for our greater good.

The nobility that fulfill the prophecy.

On page 911 of the Gideon Bible.

A folded $20 bill foretell this tragic arrival.

Though tragic it may seem, at first glance.

A deeper understanding reveals the bittersweet romance of a needed evil.

Which is beneficial toward mankind's survival. Even the hotel ground zero, called Millennium, which was designed by an enlightened individual. Gave us a clue as to what we should do.

A Space Odyssey of 2001...

But don't leave don't go. Not done.

The symbolic destruction of the pentagram in Virginia. Along with the towers of Boaz and Jachin, are seen as stargates. Our next level awaits.

Fear not,

for these are the mandates of the fates.

The fates and the graces interlace and crisscross. Just as they were for the Holocaust.

All is not lost, but found.

Bound by the blood on the innocent.

The ground receives her nourishment.

Many tears come a salty storm.

The state of Israel refound and reformed.

Here's a little break from the norm with a reason. A time of the season.

The Zionist neglected a righteous fight to gain the rite to see the site.

Land of milk and honey.

Which they now know as their own.

Their home. A prophecy shown. Shalom.
The skull & bones.
Not for power.
Not for oil.
Not even for money.
Ain't that funny. In death do we believe.
But what if we didn't....

DELIRIUM THEOREM

I hereby wish to conclude. That modern knowledge is oh, so rude.

Here,

is the

Mathematical Magick.

Divine attributes

of the

Jewish 22.™

Which I'm sure by now is nothing new to you.

Gabriel – Raphael – Gmail

Elohim:

The Supreme Being.

The inner circle.

Naturally, elementary,

Metatron

is the cube.

The cube, is the things we do.

The lines are all true.

The 10 points you already knew.

Plus the one that is hidden from view.

```
            .{Δ}.
        //   II   W̶ W̶
       //    i!     \\
      (®}.         .{↑ )
       ||           ||
      ($ }.  ii  .{ ♪ }.
       ||    @      ||
      (+ }.  ii  .{ Q)
       \\.         .//
            .(÷}.
        \\   ||   //
            .(8).
             V
             X
           iiiii
             C
```

This then one circlethenow 2.
So that the two are now 3.
A Trinity.
A divinity.
Mathematically.
Equality is a form of mathematics.

His and Her Majesty.
Rhapsody - Rasputin
Raphael - Beni - Elohim

And there you have a revolution.

Angelic operations.
Human manipulations.
Sefirah of Sofia™.
The mathematical manna.
A hint from Caprese.

Which I have to say, is not easy.
I must conclude, dare I be rude, everything we see, say, think, and do.
Alpha ~ π (w² ÷ x²) $\infty\sqrt{}$ {m},(m) ≤ Omega

ODYSSEY INCARCERATUS

DECADE THE FIRST:

Now it has become most absurd.
Ya heard! Ya heard!
I say that to say this, @theendoftheday
You just can't miss this shit.
You can't make this shit up.
Yo, my boy Bam just threw up.
He's in the slop sink all fucked up.
That good bag of dope.
Bad bag of coke.
Bag Bag it up.
He must have took one on the cuff.
Cuz the other dude had enough of Bam bullshit.
So check it, he made one up with some
rat poison. My boy Bam took one hit and started convulsing.
Enough is enough! I'm in too deep to lose it.
With all the shit I've been in. I'm in too deep to screw it.
Fuck it I blew it! I blew my freedom.
Football numbers, man I eat them'.
This Johnny Rotten Argot.
        God forsaken our God.
Ten years in. Is rotting out my brain until I'm insane.

SNOWFLAKED BARBWIRE

To the canvas of argent sky.

Snowflakes glide on the currents of changing tides. Descending from the heavens they fly.

Then become impaled by the barbwire they hide. Transforming my mind from something that once was confined. To something now free. Realizing the ironic beauty.

I stop, look, and admire their impalement,

by the barbwire.

Mnemonic legal buty. Like some sort of goofy B Movie. This crystallized spiral cryer.

The infinitely long snowflaked Barbwire.

White and free from sin, It's crystallized purity is holding me in. Yelling, free me from this fire! Redeem me of my sin!

Reflecting upon my past transgressions.

The sins that plague a penitentiary mind.

Institutions built for the benefit of mankind.

So, I search for signs to ease my mind,

and help me to find meaning in signs.

The signs of passing time.

While doing time. It was I and only I, that put me here. Subconsciously reared to face my fears.

Subconsciously, geared up.

I became corrupt. Ergo, locked up.

Shut up, in this doppelganger of society.

Altercation anxieties.

Self destruction around every nook and cranny.

I want to get back to my family,

but if someone disrespects me,

I must get at them,

IMMEDIATELY!?

Just on G.P. I mean if need be.

Letters from my family say that they need me.

The snowflakes melt exposing the barbwire once again.

HUNGARIAN GOULASH

Hungarian goulash.
Hungarian goulash.
Here in the hoosegow it's time for chow.
Hungarian goulash is on the menu!
Oh the horror, with a side of
homemade biscuits.
Massed produced product from a home I never visited. In the big house I frequenty spend my summers
and my winters.
Here in winters confinement a meal shan't be exquisite.
Your rehabilitation shall begin by changing your name into digits.
The causes of your crimes shan't never ever be illicit.
Why is this?
With no understanding of why is it.
The mind is like.
As soon as I get out of this I'm most definitely going to cause some real mischief, kid.

Yo, you want this? Nah, I'm good, kid.
The Hungarian goulash lay listless and half-eaten. Cockroaches peeking.

LA FEMME PERFUME

La Femme Perfume
that seeps through pores and creeps under cell doors.
Filling concrete with a scent.
La Femme Perfume.
The gallows await.
The seal of my fate.
My final chance for an escape.
By the neck at high noon.
Save for the moment
La Femme Perfume.

SPARROWS IN THE MESS HALL

How they fly so high, man.
I think to myself and wonder.
Why they're here, in the pen?
Then again, they really don't know they're here. Maybe we're all supposed to see and learn from them?
How to be free, while licked away in the penitentiary.

The Sun now rises to the serene scene of morning earth. Which shines the bars and alerts eyes. Then quickly back to Earth.

How can a man give birth?
By the things he says and the things he does.
Changing from what he once was to what he has now become.
A change.
A break.
A heavenly place.
Yes I made mistakes.
Yes I ate of the tree, naturally.
But why do I feel guilty?
To put it simply. If naturally, I was born corrupted then why do I feel interrupted by shame? Who's to blame?
The one who created this falsehood.
Should I not believe I am a child of God.
Does that sound odd?
Does that sound strange?
Maybe my freewill made me change.
Like an angel the sparrow flies out the of the mess hall of this penitentiary and to the skies of the heavens. Like unleavened bread. I was once dead, but now I'm alive. Show me how to live?

GOD TIME AND A RHYME

God gave me time to give me time.
Sitting in my cell I manifest this rhyme.
It's a thin line between fake and real.
Learned that fact when I took the D.A's deal.
So I guess my fate is sealed.
Many call it kismet.
How long will I have to deal with all this, that, and the third bullshit?
Sitting back thinking deep while my cigarette lit.
Maybe I should just go legit?
Then again, a voice in my head says that sounds like stupid shit.
I just wish I could get rid of all this pain from past sorrows.
Hoping on some kind of better tomorrow.
This time I think I'll follow a different
path, the narrow path.
Caught up in the rapture.
Captured by Satan's grip.
I think maybe, I could slip through the cracks.
I know God's got my back, and I'll never lack nuffin'. So best stop frontin' and say something.
Please God, forgive me for all the sins
I done did. Didn't mean to hurt no one.
I understand why you gave up your life for us.
Sometimes when I talk I cuss.
So forgive me for all those times I acted nutz.
I don't mean to fuss, but watch over my family. If I get in trouble sending the calvary.
I pray this prayer bended knee.
Now I see. Now I know. From the highest high to the lowest low.
The first, the last, the only, true God.
Even though a lot of people think you're odd,
To me, you're always the same.
In the name of the word, and all that you have heard, Amen.

THE WEIGHT OF WAIT

I wait in this self induced separation.

With schoolgirl anticipation.

For my loves dissertation.

Which has been decreed onto me by the Almighty.

An angel from heaven who waits for me.

Time ticks on me like a ton of inquiries.

Worries squeezing at the beats of my heart.

Lost in the darkness of this incarcerated incapacitated abyss.

Man, how I miss her blissful kisses.

Remnants of which are sent on letters of passionate ink and sealed with a kiss. (s.w.a.k)

I read and think and sink deeper and deeper

into the weight of our next correspondence.

Medieval transponder, in the midst of the opulent age of technological advances.

I wait, in concrete circumstances.

Awaiting the chance to hear my name on a piece of mail.

Then once again can soul can set sail.

Imagine the weight a letter takes on.

When waiting on mail is your only escape.

So, till then I weight.

NOCTURNAL INQUISITION

Night settles in and my thoughts start to wonder once again.

Drifting on the currents of this nocturnal Inquisition.

Pushed forth by my willingness to be

the bearer of light.

Up all night.

Trying to reveal the unseen blockades.

Giving shade to the shadeless and giving light to that which holds me back.

Another dimension to my illuminated destination.

The clocks sweeps while comfort sleeps. While I stay arised with wide opened eyes.

Believing my own lies.

Mesmerised, hypnotized by the stars of this curiously darken sky.

The incarcerated sights and sounds of concrete vibrations bounce off these walls reverberating myself examination.

Hallucinations?

An inmate's lullaby.™

I stare as the frigid air chillaxes my anxiety.

Hopes and dreams seem to far from me.

And now this curiously darken sky becomes diluted with bits of morning light.

Turning a dark blue, white.

Up all night.

Am I the dream?

Is this the dream?

How can I fulfill my dream scapeescape,

if I can't even rest in peace?

THE SILENCE OF
FALLING TREES

In the forest of my faults.

A fearless tree falls.

Crush by the regular rush with an irregular hush. In accordance with the law.

That's when this tree falls.

By the gavel to the ground.

Barely a sound.

The sound judgement of Justice.

Just us people.

In suit and tie.

Help me to see why?

Help me to see why I try.

So vehemently to return to the penitentiary

again and again? A round trip release date in my head and in my hand. Already making plans that
get me back here again. As soon as I can.

Trying to understand understanding.

Because where I come from, going to jail is a man thing. Getting over is definitely not a bad thing.

A legend of the streets.

That'll make your ears ring,

When there's trouble afoot.

That'll make your eyes sting.

A tree was cut down.

A mighty tree of nine rings.

When it hit the ground you heard neither

sigh nor wince. Soundless as the wind.

BARRY SANDERS PHILOSOPHY

The defense is ready.
Armed to the teeth with their criticizing machetes. Ready to slice.
I move left

I move right

Stop on a dime because I'm just that nice.
Got them thinking twice.
Life is a lot like a football game.
Sometimes you gotta switch the direction of your aim.
Like switching lanes. Regression your progression. Sometimes you gotta keep them guessing. Keep them stressing so their next move will be with frustration. The way is not always a straight line.

      Zag

Zig.

Back pedal.
Gather up steam and hit that daylight hot like a tea kettle.
Barry baby.
Sometimes you gotta be like a lion who waits for just the right moment.
Waiting to pounce, and when it happens.
You better own it!
Gray or Blue?
Don't let you, stop you!
The best defense we play against is our your own brain.
Reverse on your guilt.
Reverse on your pain.
Reverse on the way you play the blame game.
Have faith and believe in every inch you achieve. If you go backwards take heed in these words.
Sometimes you gotta go backwards to move forwards.

The
Barry Sanders philosophy
#20 G.O.A.T.

BIBLICAL GRAFFITI

Dig this scene if you will:

Lamenting in a jail cell that's not very clean. The walls are painted a high yellow stagnant brown green. With the pungent stench of urine and sin. Locus odor de toilette.

Without & within and then, there is that which I am lamenting in.

My sentencing.

Not from a magistrate of any court, you see, but rather, the reasoning behind why.

Why did my dear Mother choose not to abort me?

This be the tale of how I failed, and yet at the same time prevailed with perfect reception.

A humble recognition for this illustrious life I have been given. Admission of this was a twist of my wrist. A slice and a kiss.

Which is not as easy as one might wish. The reason being. I refused believing that my life has meaning. Seeing this situation as such, put me in quite the rut. I must admit, I became an insatiable nut. So I made a knot. Then fashioned it into a noose. Then I chose a nice place where it wouldn't come loose. Excuse after excuse for and against. Made the whole situation extremely intense.

And then...

"Lights out!"

The C.O. just shouts.

It's time. The 11th hour and no one, but no one is moving about. So I quickly grab my noose from whereabouts I had it hiding out. Then tired about at the top of my jail cell. At just about the right height in the darkness of the night. Nothing but the moonlight guiding my site.

Over my head, right right?

Nice and tight, right right?

Alright.

JUMP OFF THE BUNK!!!

Plunk and then I sunk. A shortness of breath. No life left? Then I feel the clock hit 12. What in the hell?! Dizzy now, I wasn't feeling very well.

I must have fell.

The noose broke.

What the hell!

The moonlight in the cell catches my attention. As it shines on an etching of biblical graffiti. No doubt put there by the inmate before me. Trying to warn me or encourage. My mind is nervous. Feels like I'm in service. In some sort of service. Gasping for air. I look and I stare. Right there before my eyes, to my very surprise, the answer that cures this suicidal cancer, FOREVER.

Be that light that you seek.

Be that Beacon for all to see.

So people like you and people like me can find a way, a way to be free.

If all that doesn't work.

For a good time just

call Stacy. Her head game is KZ,

ODYSSEY INCARCERATUS

One minute left.

1 minutes to go.

Before everything I knew and everything I know, will be nothing but a bad rerun. A bad memory show. 25 years of penitentiary fears. Dried up tears that made my face rough and made my mind numb. The ultra-violence of this sanctimonious sanctum. Caused all my dreams bleed out of me like a wilted rose.

I have stained so many D.O.C bed sheets. Now my time is close.

A bloody nose I suppose from all who opposed me. Down the road I hope to feel those freedom bed sheets again. Those made of silk, satin, and cotton. All the beautiful things that I have long forgotten. An old Con's dream. A Bud Light scene. An old man's dream of the family thing. Something, all to far. From where we are. From where I live. Now set free from the delinquent's emporium. With an irregular equilibrium. An irregular plot and an irregular scheme. Go out and get me some. Because where I come from, you got to have something to be someone.

25 years later.
I lost all my family and all my friends.
Just me on these streets, and I got to eat.
So here we go hands and feet.
In 30 seconds I'll be free.

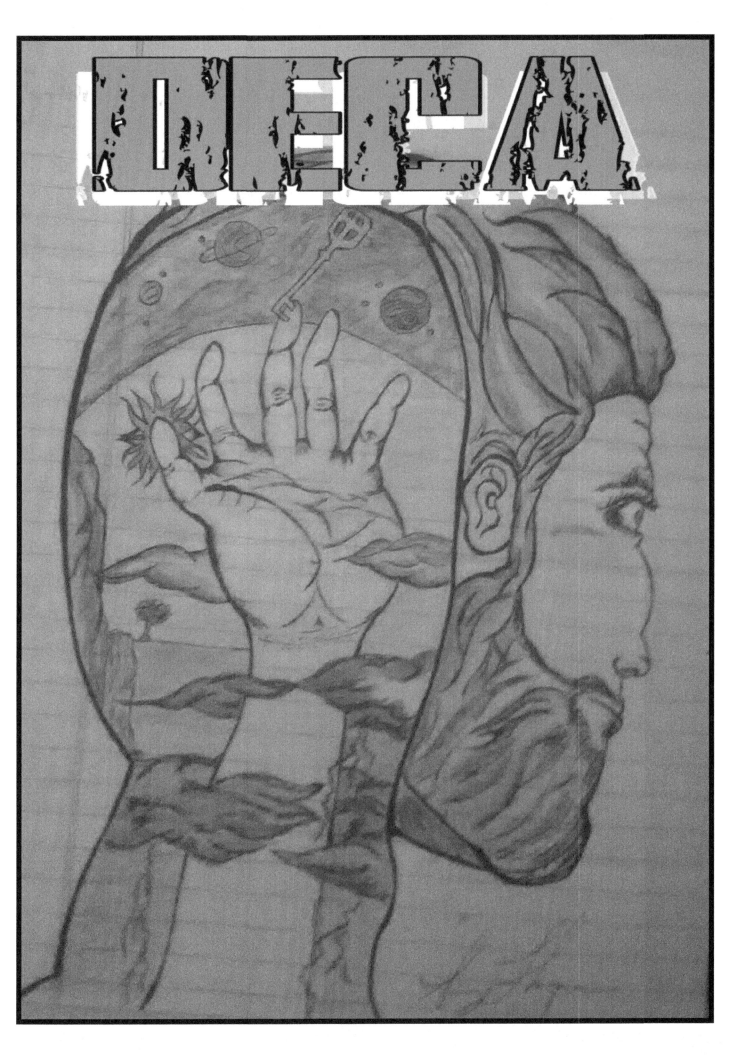

ROBIN WILLIAMS

Mork from Ork your mind was fantastically berserk.
I remember your first stand-up routine.
What a chaotic scene.
The bewildering hilarious gleam
into the mind of a comic genius.
Unchained, on stage.
All amused and amazed by the characters you played.
We fail to see the veil you kept.
Hidden.
Hiding.
Hunger for that big sleep.
Now we are left with nothing but
a silver screen and the shadows of something so scary, so true, that behind the joys, behind the laughs,
behind a smile and someone clap. There lays a why. Deep down inside. That will eat to your core.
Till the day that you die.

IT

Life is what you make of
it.
That's why I think about taking
it.
I'm just going through the motions.
Like I'm faking
it.
Just anticipating
it.
Something in my life just don't fit. All this
it.
Sit down and take a minute and let me explain
it.
It's my peerless situation.
It's my deep depression.
That eats at my soul, and I long for my body to turn cold.
Now, I know what you have been told.
You won't see the other side if you commit suicide.
But I can no longer hide from
it.
Fuck
it!
Let this blade release the crimson gush rushing freedom from sorrow and pain.
As I write this, my tears fall like rain.
I can't believe I can't get this out of my brain?
My heart yells "Sustain!, Sustain!"
Why am I complaining about
it?
Why don't I just get up and do
it?
I don't know, maybe this is a cry for help from
it.

ATTACK OF THE ATOMIC ZOMBIES FROM BIKINI ISLAND

Greetings Bob, I'm here on the scene, at my job. Interviewing this poor slob. Who, by golly, is about to witness the Almighty H–Bomb, as it's called. It will soon bombard this here Island of Bikini. With all sorts of spooky gigahertz radioactive frequencies. I believe some sort of Einstein equation ejaculation. An Oppenheimer Foundation. Truly Bob, A deflowering detonation to say the least. Well anyway, like I was saying, I'm here interviewing Raimi Savini. Who just happens to be the Roger of this here Corman of Bikini. He will also be the only civilian witness to feel the mighty force of the new and improved atomic bomb up close and personal. From where we are standing we can see the beautiful

Crystal Plumage Pageantry of the atoll.

Raimi, may I call you Raimi?

I much rather prefer Mister Savini.

Okay, Mr. Savini. What say you?

What in the name of Carpenter Craven! Why are you guys doing this to me? This is insane. Can you guys untie these strings holding me in.

Set me free! What in the hell are you guys doing to me? Please, please let me be!

Bava Fulci, now. For the Mother of tears, Argento! Those are not strings, but rather MK Vines holding you in. A Killer Tomatoes and Georgie Romero. Untie yourself if you want, but if you do. No big ads bomb for you.

Jesus, Franco! Takashi Miike!

What's that moving in the distance far away?

Look it's moving with great speed on a path of least resistance. Headed straight for Raimi Savini! OMG! Is that a Zombie!?

Cannibal Terror o'plenty.

Deep in the jungle the flesh-eaters are waiting.

Well Bob, it looks like there's no need in hesitating. All hope is lost and we're better off dead. Hey Ed, Wood you get a nice tight shot of that zombie eating Mr. Saving's flesh. I digress. As I look to the sky, Tarantino to the west, I can now see the bomb as it makes it's descent. Hey get this, there appears to be what looks like a man straddling the bomb as it makes its way down. Yes. Yes, he is riding it!

Waving a flag or some sort of bonnet...

CONFESSIONS OF
SAINT GERMAIN

Here I am.

Here I was.

Here I shall forever be.

As you can see, the complexity of my immortality is the combination of a discipline in physics, a hint of religious fundamentalist, and a dash of good old insanity. Which brew well in the Temple.

Beneath me is the foundry.

A cauldron of illuminated alchemy.

A roller coaster romance of happenstance. Oligarchic blossoms bloom with the heritage of deep purple. Sacrificed upon virgin crimson.

Her eyes,

wide shut by disbelief.

Strangled by the grief of her impending demise. Lies told by her master.

A comfortable disaster.

Her name is Society.

Her master, Separation.

The litigation of doubt causes a drought of an intellectuals blossoming out.

The reroute blackout.

We have a decision!

We have made a decision!

It's a technical knockout!

Yes, Yes!

An amazing blow delivered by the mighty Whitey and his picket fence!

Pow right in the kiss her!

If you had your chance?

If you know the way?

If you know all the right words and just what to say?

Would you stay on this plain for all of eternity?

Or would you much rather be harmoniously eturnel?

SUPPLICATIONS OF A MAGNANIMOUS CRIMINAL

To ask, or not to ask?

This is my question.

Since I took the time to ask,

I shall take my time, to answer.

Forgiveness?

To be forgiven?

If the meaning is in the feeling for the need to be, then I know this not.

This quixotic mission delivered by the hand of infancy.

Has fashioned me to be, the hope of Gandhi, the pride of John Brown, and the admiration of Simon Cowell.

I drink of the cup of the Garden of Gethsemane, and when it's empty, I ask for more.

Here upon the shore of long suffering.

Engulfed by barbwire and concrete.

I watch the sun set on human morality.

I begin to contemplate those lives drowning in the shallow sea of self-pity.

Oh how I do pity those who are lost and asking for forgiveness.

I reflect upon myself, many a time.

Rhyming for reasons. Bittersweet seasons.

A taste for perfection.

A quest for the question.

My earthly journey for the unseen, unanswered, unimaginable
abstract obligations to the eye of God.

All the while whimsical wallops of whimpers and whines. Graciously granted to me by man eyed steeples. Obstruct the views from the peoples. These same peoples were taught to be fearful of their own spiritual gifts.

Our own immaculate perception.

Their stagnant waters fester,

Talkie, no Walkie.

Gossip fornicators with reservations for one.

Forbid me not to rob them all blind, deaf, and dumb!

The sum of all my summations, shall be the knowledge of the Angelic jewels cultivated by department store orphans and wild turkey hobos.

As the sky transforms her color scheme,

The Sun quickly slips to a distant dream, and The Night of Shrouded Chaos, anticipates his arrival.

I am thankful for my little China.

My precious daughter who I have yet to see.

Though I know her answer is one and the same, just like me.

Supplications of a magnanimous criminal.

THE COMPOSITION D'COPULATION

Our introduction:

In a momentary glance
which feels like an extended version of romance.
Our flirtatious dances of
smiles and chances.
From across the room our eyes happen to meet. Hungry eyes now complete.
The libretto begins
with the undertones of sin
the overtones are
vocal pheromones.
Acousticophilia ear bone.
She whispers unto me,
the sweet heat rhapsody,
ravish me!
Eyes burn with intensity
rollback in ecstasy.
A slight staccato.
A pounding Allegro.
Sinfonia gasmic,
rhythm and temple.
A heart beat arpeggio.
The sweat beads
virtuoso.
Our symphony,
this symphony,
sacred secretions,
releasing inhibitions.
Injecting the essence,
And releasing resistance.
The soloists have now become the orchestra of each other.
The reverberation of new lovers.
Inward verse inverses into outward intuitions.
We changing positions in unison.
Here in the rhythms of each other we find utopia.
The deep dark magenta of night remixes
into the soft bright cyan of first morning light.
Collaborating sensations.
Calibrating stimulations.

Internal combustion!
Simultaneous eruption!

We are set free!
In this moment.
This magnificent aria of
You & Me.
A copulating symphony.

RAZOR WIRE STATIC

Twisting and turning.
This razor wire static is blaring.
Blurring my rites to get it right.
I lite my spice at night.
K2 mountain height.
Blue caution mountain flight.
Occurring and reoccurring.
Tossing and turning.
My ill-willed mind, can't stay still.
Spitting on the gate about argot thrills and
a hell-bent mission for fool's gold and cheap pills. The razor wire static that once enchanted me. Is now converted into a very low frequency. That eats at me bowels.
Causing vomit.
I calm down, and take another puff on it.
Then I press play.
The combination makes my mind sway.
Placating my soul and quieting my qualms.

The sweet rhythm of a hard beat.

Like a heartbeat that softens the concrete.

These steel bars vibrate to the sound of violins, horn sections, church organs,

and a cold guitar with a hot lick.

I think after 25 years in a few minutes I'll be free.
The sounds in the mind and this killer beat.

How to find ends meat?

When I leave this prison where will they send me? No friends, no family, nowhere to run when times get tough on me.
25 years of penitentiary.
I don't even think I know how to shop for groceries.

THE AMBER DOOR

Behind the Amber door,
Love burns a lonely desire, eversore.
Separated nights adorned with starry lights.
A lonely night aglow with scorn.
Wandering minds that implicate love crimes.
Behind the Amber door, she finds herself.
Intertwines herself to find herself.
She minds herself to the memories of cheesy one liners and cheap wine.
A silly little love that she never minds.
Now that it's gone, out of sight, forever blind.
Behind The Amber door her love is dry.

CONVERSATION VERTIGO

Selfie grams/
it's selfie grams/
In these pics I'm selfie stamped/
#emojiland/
With these pics I take a stand/
Everywhere I go I take a stand/
Conversation vertigo/

If you like what I say/
well, let me know/
If you don't/
then you're a troll/

This is how we mind control/
Conversation vertigo/
Free to say what you want to say/
As long as you say/
what I want you to say/
That's the way we instachat/
She changed her face to instant kitty cat/
Deleted pictures of her on her back/
Conversation vertigo/

If you like what I say/
well, let me know/
If you don't/
then you're a troll/

This is how we mind control/
Conversation vertigo/
This all started many many years ago/
The good folks of Babel/
A Creator slammed his gavel/
and created gobble gabble/
Many different words/
with many different meaning/
Praise be he/
The Benevolent Being/
Conversation vertigo/

If you like what I say/
well, let me know/
If you don't/
then you're a troll/

This is how we mind control/
Conversation vertigo/

PSYCHOSOMATICA

Hereunder.
Hereto.
Herein lies.

        The conflict
        betwixt and between
        the soul and the body.

Nobody knows the trouble I seen.♪
Nobody know my sorrow.♪
Today and the morrow
all blend together.

        'Tweather night or day
        all is one,
        continuously,
        repetitiously,

Lang Sangral of a day.
Dare I speak,
the 6th day,
of the 6th month,
of the 6th year,
of the 21st century.
And lo,
appeared unto me a Beelzebee.
Buzzing in my ear
A harem-scarem.
From here to there
and everywhere.
And who, and what, and when.

        And then me thinkest,
"That this is something of the sort of Tempest which is trying to suggest that I steer clear of the whirling violent wind from this here, Beelzebee.
He Witch we cannot see, but indubitably we feel!"

Theretofore, I was still able to maintain some stability,
in the brain,
in the mind theirin.
Then again,
my body starts to shiver,
every time l holdest in my frustration.

My first inclination,

to freest me from this frustration

was to lay hold of the aggravating aggravation,

and rebuke the tempest temptation,

and all it's medieval machinations it has cast before me…"

And then methinkest,

"Now that, that would be complete and utter insanity and they would probably put me in something

of the sort of padded room with no room but to lyest upon a cot all day and all…

Not! Not gonna do it! Screw it!"

I fell for it.

What any good red blooded Amerigo

"like whatever"

Nose.

To show who is the bigger foe.

Fee, fi, fo, fum,

I smell the fear of a Middle Eastern.

And thereafter,

The hereafter…

Year after year,

in the constant conflict

of the wouldest I couldest

have done something different

to just have some fun,

and not hurt no one,

especially myself.

Instead I lay upon this shelf, collecting dust in disgust of some dumb thing I did way back when, and

how I'm going to change all my ways.

Stuck the haze from this day daze.

Strange this maze.

Just when you think you made it out…

It pulls you back in!

How could this one ever win!

How could that one ever achieve!

How could…

Look, out there in the audience?

People!!! Ahaaaaaaaaaaaa!!!

INT: CONVENIENCE STORE- EARLY

A FREE MAN'S ODYSSEY

WE SEE **OUR HERO** enter the convenience store in a panic course. The reason for his anxious ways. It seems his mind is in a daze.

Made that way by blinking fluorescent tubes and stupid ass boobs who drag their feet.

Making way too much noise with their fucking shoes!

Plus, it's **OUR HERO's** first day free.

After a quarter of a century in the penitentiary. It shows on his face like the stench of fresh meat.

OUR HERO: (V.O.)

What can I do?
Split his skull and take his shoes?
Just stained red my one and two?
Women and children crying blue?
Call the Jake, red and blue?
Escape mistake?
Take the train 4 0 2?
Sentencing 2 to 4?
Open the door back
to cell block 4?
Another statistic
forevermore?
So many choices.
So many fucking choices,
of soft drinks to drink!
This one here is for energy and this one right here, this one gives you clarity. I think?
And to think of it.
135 different kinds of soft drinks, and not a one of them do I know how to drink.
I want to have a drink.
Fucking lights that blink!
This store is way too fucking bright.
25 years of sleeping alone.
Alone again tonight.
Need some cash

for that sweet little lady of the night.
Tonight's the night. Tonight I'm free bady.
Free at last! free at last!..
I wonder how long this will last?

Fade Out

Printed in the United States
By Bookmasters